Hernando Cortés
and the Conquest of Mexico

Explorers of New Worlds

Hernando Cortés
and the Conquest of Mexico

Gina De Angelis

Chelsea House Publishers
Philadelphia

MS
BIO
COL

1/04

Prepared for Chelsea House Publishers by:
OTTN Publishing, Warminster, PA

CHELSEA HOUSE PUBLISHERS
Editor in Chief: Stephen Reginald
Production Manager: Pamela Loos
Managing Editor: James D. Gallagher
Art Director: Sara Davis
Director of Photography: Judy L. Hasday
Senior Production Editor: LeeAnne Gelletly
Series Designer: Keith Trego

5 7 9 8 6 4

Library of Congress Cataloging-in-Publication Data

DeAngelis, Gina.
    Hernando Cortés / by Gina DeAngelis.
64 p.   cm. – (Explorers of new worlds)
Includes bibliographical references and index.
Summary: A biography of the explorer whose brutal conquest of the Aztecs in Mexico was responsible for the first
Spanish settlements in the New World.
ISBN 0-7910-5516-7 (hc)
1. Cortés, Hernán 1485-1547 Juvenile literature. 2. Mexico–History–Conquest, 1519-1540 Juvenile literature. 3.
Mexico–Discovery and exploration–Spanish Juvenile literature. 4. Conquerors–Mexico Biography Juvenile literature. 5. Explorers–Mexico–Biography Juvenile literature. 6. Explorers–Spain–Biography Juvenile literature.
[1. Cortés, Hernando, 1485-1547. 2. Explorers. 3. Mexico–History–Conquest, 1519-1540.] I. Title. II. Series.
F1230.C835D4   1999
972'.02'092–dc21   99-35232
[B]   CIP

Contents

The City
in a Lake

Tenochtitlán, the capital of the Aztec empire, was a beautiful city in the center of a lake. The city was connected to the mainland by long roads across the water, called causeways. About 150,000 Aztecs lived in the city when Hernando Cortés and his men arrived there in 1519.

I

On November 8, 1519, a bearded man on horseback took up position at the head of a column of several hundred soldiers. For months the soldiers had been marching across difficult, dangerous territory, and all but a handful of them were on foot. But on this day their spirits were high. For just five miles ahead, at the end of a **causeway** (a raised road that crosses water), lay their destination: a beautiful city in the middle of a lake. That city,

Tenochtitlán (Ten-OCH-tit-lan), was the capital of a vast, powerful empire and held untold riches.

Hernando Cortés, the bearded man at the head of the column, was the leader of the soldiers. A Spaniard, like the men who followed him, Cortés had a lifelong dream of adventure, glory, and riches. Now in his mid-thirties, he seemed on the brink of fulfilling that dream. The powerful Aztecs, a tribe that ruled over much of the central part of what is now Mexico, had invited Cortés and his men into Tenochtitlán.

The city, built on an island in Lake Texcoco, was connected to the mainland by causeways with removable pieces that left large gaps when they were moved. The gaps let canoes cross through the causeways. They also kept enemies from entering the city. An *aqueduct* carried fresh water from the mainland to the city's inhabitants for drinking, bathing, and irrigation. Tenochtitlán also had bustling marketplaces, huge temples, ball courts, public plazas, and beautiful gardens, not to mention *suburbs* along the shores of Lake Texcoco.

No one knows exactly where the Aztecs came from originally. According to their own legends, they left their homeland in 1168. They then entered the Valley of Mexico (the high plateau in the central part of the country) and spent about 100 years wandering before they settled around Lake Texcoco. At this time they probably numbered only a few thousand, and the more powerful tribes in the area forced them onto the least desirable swampland.

But a century after the founding of Tenochtitlán in 1325, the Aztecs had gained power by making alliances and serving as *mercenaries* (paid soldiers) for other native groups in the area. By about the mid-1400s, the Aztecs had conquered their neighbors. Their strong and efficient army was feared throughout the Valley of Mexico and beyond.

While their armies were conquering, the Aztecs' civilization grew more complex. The Aztecs required all children, male and female, to attend schools. They were the only people in the world to provide

Tenochtitlán was founded in 1325 when the wandering Aztecs saw a cactus growing from a split rock. On the cactus perched an eagle, wings spread, with a snake in its mouth. (Today, this image appears on Mexico's flag.) The Aztec priests thought this was a sign that they should build their empire on the site.

Cortés and his men enter Tenochtitlán in this Spanish painting, as anxious Aztecs paddle past the causeway.

public education to all. Specialized professions arose. Trade flourished, and the Aztecs collected **tribute** (goods or money demanded by a conquering people in exchange for safety) from the peoples they defeated, which made their society wealthy. Aztec artisans and craftsmen created beautiful works of art and made Tenochtitlán a magnificent capital.

As Hernando Cortés and his soldiers marched across the causeway toward Tenochtitlán that November morning, the Spaniards were awed by the city's beauty. Sunlight glimmered off the waves in the lake. Lime-plastered walls glowed a bright white in the sun. Huge pyramid-shaped buildings housed temples to the Aztec gods, including their fierce war god, Huitzilopochtli. And with a population of about 150,000, Tenochtitlán was bigger than any European city at the time.

Many men would have thought twice before leading such a small army—fewer than 500 soldiers— into the very heart of a powerful empire. But Hernando Cortés was a shrewd and ambitious man eager for adventure, glory, and, most of all, riches. And ever since his expedition had landed on the Yucatán **Peninsula** earlier in the year, natives had told the Spaniards about the Aztecs' fabulous wealth.

Cortés had gotten a taste of this wealth when messengers sent by the Aztec emperor, Montezuma, had come to him bearing gifts of gold. The promise of more riches drowned out any fears the Spanish leader may have had and drew him forward to Tenochtitlán.

Cortés didn't know it, but his long journey from the coast inland to the Aztec capital had been greatly aided by luck. Aztec prophecies and omens had seemed to foretell his arrival, and Montezuma thought that the white-skinned leader might be a god.

According to an Aztec legend, the gentle god Quetzalcoatl (the Feathered Serpent) had opposed the sacrifices of human blood made to the other Aztec gods, especially Huitzilopochtli. Quetzalcoatl had taught the Aztec people the arts of farming, weaving, writing, and pottery. But, centuries before Montezuma's time, Quetzalcoatl had been chased from the land by the other gods. He had promised to return one day to rule over his people. According to Aztec beliefs, at the end of every 52-year calendar cycle there was great danger that the world would end unless the gods were appeased with offerings of human blood. The Aztec year One Reed was at the end of one such 52-year cycle. It was also the year Quetzalcoatl would return, the prophets said. By coincidence, One Reed corresponded with the year 1519–the year Cortés arrived.

Paintings of this god showed him as a man with white skin and a black beard, who came from the direction of the sunrise (east). All of this fit the description of Cortés.

There were other signs that trouble might be brewing for Montezuma's people. In the months before Cortés's landing, a comet had appeared in the sky. Huge waves on Lake Texcoco flooded homes in Tenochtitlán. Elders reported horrible dreams of destruction. The temple of Huitzilopochtli was struck by lightning. The volcano Popocatepetl began to rumble and smoke. And some people in the city claimed to hear a woman's voice crying in the night, foretelling doom.

These omens troubled Montezuma. He couldn't decide what to do when messengers brought news that white-skinned strangers had arrived along the coast in large floating houses with wings (sailing ships). They carried sticks that seemed able to produce both thunder and flashes like lightning. They had huge fighting dogs, larger than any known in Mexico. Even stranger were the horses, which the native peoples had never seen before.

As the days and weeks went by, the news that Montezuma's messengers brought became more

The Aztec emperor Montezuma kneels before Cortés,
greeting the Spanish conquistador with gifts. The ruler of
Tenochtitlán believed Cortés might be a god.

ominous. Cortés and his soldiers made their way inland, defeating the local peoples who stood in their way. The white-skinned strangers were horrified by the religious practices of the native peoples, which included **human sacrifice**. Quetzalcoatl, of course, didn't like human sacrifice either. Montezuma was even more upset to learn that fierce groups like the Tlaxcalans, whom the Aztecs had not been able to conquer, were being badly beaten by just a few of these mysterious white men. They were also abandoning their gods for the whites' religion.

Believing that Cortés might be Quetzalcoatl, Montezuma hoped the god would bless his people and leave. As the Spaniards neared Tenochtitlán, he sent magnificent gifts to honor the "god" and asked Cortés not to enter Tenochtitlán. But Cortés had no intention of turning back—particularly after seeing the gold Montezuma had sent.

If Montezuma had acted decisively, the Aztecs probably could have defeated the hopelessly outnumbered Spaniards in battle. But he wavered, finally inviting the white men into his capital. When the soldiers entered Tenochtitlán, the emperor greeted them. He was probably wondering just who the figure at the head of the group was—man or god.

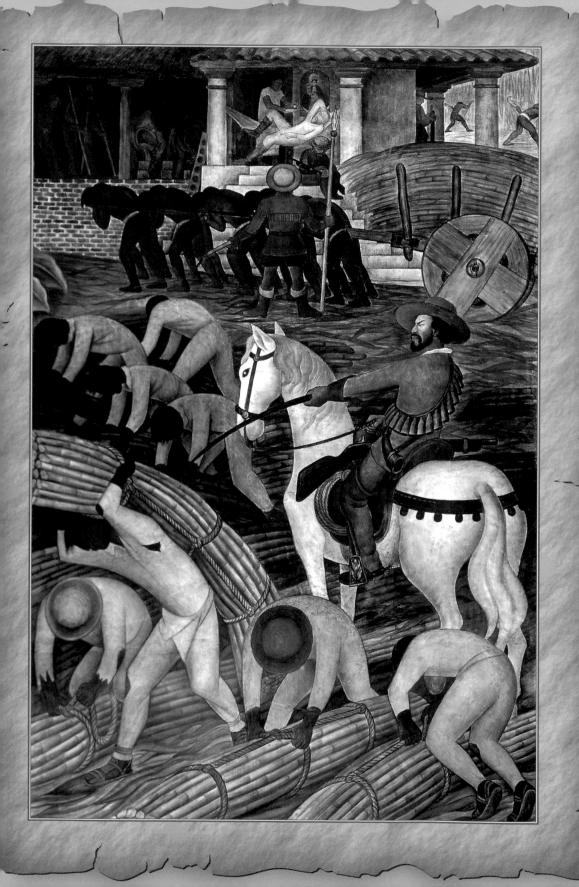

When the Spanish arrived in the New World, they often mistreated and enslaved the natives, as is shown in this painting of a Spanish overseer directing slaves on a sugar plantation.

Who Was Hernando Cortés?

2

*H*ernando (or, in some sources, Hernán) Cortés was born in 1485 in Medellín, a town in the Spanish *province* known as Extremadura. This area, near the present-day border of Portugal, was the poorest part of Spain. Farming was so hard that most young men there decided to seek their fortune as soldiers. In fact, many of Spain's most famous *conquistadors* came from Extremadura.

The Cortés family, though of noble rank, was neither rich nor poor. Cortés's father was a former cavalry officer, and his mother was a very devout Catholic. As a child, Cortés was often sick, but he grew up to be very healthy.

In 1499, at the age of 14, he went to the University of Salamanca to study law. In later years Cortés was considered something of a scholar, so he may have done well at school. But after about two years of study, Cortés became bored and restless. He returned home and got himself into some trouble involving women. His parents worried that he would not amount to much.

During Cortés's youth, Spain had become a world power. Two large kingdoms on the Iberian Peninsula were united by the marriage of King Ferdinand of Aragon and Queen Isabella of Castile. This formed the modern nation of Spain. The new nation was fiercely Catholic. In 1492, when Cortés was seven years old, Spanish armies drove the **Moors** out of Spain. The Moors, North Africans who followed the religion Islam, had ruled the peninsula for centuries.

But in 1492 another event occurred that was just as important for the Spanish: Christopher Columbus discovered many islands in the Caribbean. Although Columbus assumed the islands he reached were off the coast of China, he had actually stumbled upon the "New World."

By the early 1500s, the people of Europe were just beginning to find their way around the globe.

Moorish soldiers ride off to war in this 13th century Arabian fresco. The Moors were finally forced out of Spain in 1492. This freed the Spanish rulers to expand their empire by exploring and conquering the New World.

Spain and Portugal competed to be the first to plunder the riches of the new lands, to plant colonies and develop trade, and to convert the natives that lived there to Christianity.

Cortés was sure his destiny (or at least some adventure) lay in the New World. He dreamed, like many conquistadors, of growing rich and finding glory there. In 1504, when he was 19, he boarded a supply ship to travel to the new Spanish settlement on the island of Hispaniola.

Hernando Cortés came from a noble family, but one with little money or power. From a young age, he was interested in adventure. He hoped to find it on Hispaniola.

It was a long, difficult trip. The ship's main mast broke in a storm and had to be repaired at the Canary Islands. Then the captain lost his way, fresh water and food ran low, and the ship encountered more storms. Fortunately for the crew, a dove was eventually spotted. The ship followed the bird to arrive safely at the port town of Santo Domingo in Hispaniola.

This eventful voyage did not tame Cortés's restless spirit. As a noble, he was offered land where he could settle. He replied that he had come to find gold and riches, not to till the soil like a peasant. But there was little else he could do at the time, so young Cortés became a sugar planter in the colony on Hispaniola.

In Spanish colonies in the New World, when a settler was granted land, he was also given responsibility for the native people who lived on it. The settler was supposed to supply the natives with food and see that they got a Christian education so that they could be converted. In return, the natives had to work for the settler. This unfair arrangement was called the **encomienda** system. It was supposed to replace slavery, but it often amounted to pretty much the same thing. Thousands of natives died from starvation and overwork at the hands of the **encomenderos**, or landowners.

For seven years Cortés lived on Hispaniola as a sugar planter. Although he prospered, he never gave up his dreams of adventure.

Hispaniola was one of the first islands discovered by Christopher Columbus in 1492. He called it *La Isla Espanola*–the Spanish Isle. It was the site of Spain's first colony in the New World. Today, the island is shared by two nations: Haiti and the Dominican Republic.

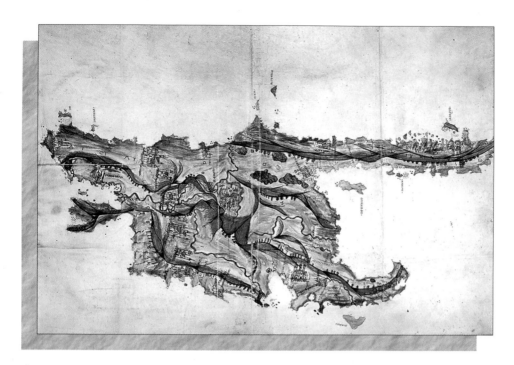

The small island of Hispaniola had been discovered by Christopher Columbus. Cortés spent his first few years in the New World living near a town Columbus founded, Santo Domingo. He helped the Spaniards enslave the natives of the island before moving on to Cuba in 1511.

In 1511 he sailed with another wealthy Hispaniola landowner, Diego Velásquez de Cuellar, on an expedition to conquer the island of Cuba.

Their invasion was a success. Velásquez was made governor of Cuba, and Cortés was given land and slaves. He also married a young Spanish woman named Catalina Xuárez (or Juárez), a relative of Velásquez. Cortés raised livestock on his vast estate, spent a lot of money, and served as Velásquez's assistant.

During his time in Cuba, Cortés got into some trouble. He was suspected of plotting to overthrow Velásquez and was thrown in prison. He escaped twice. Finally he settled down and focused on running his estate. All the while he hoped someday to be given permission to explore and conquer.

Finally, in 1518, after seven years in Cuba, he was chosen to lead the second official expedition to Yucatán (as Mexico was then known). Velásquez had sent an expedition to Yucatán earlier that year to investigate reports of an advanced civilization living there. That expedition, commanded by Juan de Grijalva, had stayed only long enough to learn that Yucatán was not an island. Cortés was supposed to explore, to make contact with the natives, and to convert them to Christianity.

Caught up in this new adventure, Cortés spent much of his own money on the ships and supplies and busied himself recruiting men. At some point, though, Velásquez started to regret his choice of leaders. The reasons aren't known today, but the governor decided to relieve Cortés of his command. Cortés simply ignored Velásquez's orders.

Converting the natives of the New World to Christianity was very important to the Spaniards. Catholic Europe believed that at the time of Christ's Second Coming, the whole world should be Christian to meet him. Also, they believed, a person could get into heaven by bringing the "true faith" to new people.

He hurriedly assembled his crews, loaded his ships, and even looted the governor's slaughterhouse.

In February 1519, Cortés's fleet set sail for Yucatán. Eleven ships carried more than 500 soldiers and 100 sailors. The ships also carried kegs of wine and drinking water, supplies of beans, bread and flour, live chickens and pigs (for meat), crossbows and muskets, 14 cannon with powder and shot, swords and lances, and 16 horses.

The small fleet ran into storms that damaged some ships. But the real danger, the Spaniards knew, would come on their arrival in Yucatán. There they would encounter warlike natives who had routed the first Spaniards to land in the area. In 1517 a slave-gathering party led by Hernández de Córdoba had landed on the Yucatán Peninsula by accident. Only half of the Spaniards had escaped with their lives. But the survivors had brought back tales of gold and other treasures.

Cortés's men may have known that not all of them would survive either. But the thought of that gold—mountains of it, enough to make a man wealthy beyond imagination—pushed them along.

Conquest

Hernando Cortés orders his men to burn their ships before setting forth to conquer the Aztec Empire. He hoped to inspire his soldiers to fight harder by doing this, because without ships they would have no way to leave Mexico. The Spaniards were facing a daunting task: their force of under 500 was pitted against an empire of three million Aztecs.

3

When Cortés's fleet arrived at the island of Cozumel, off the east coast of the Yucatán Peninsula, the explorers met friendly people. The island may have been a designated peaceful trading area. Cortés thought there might be Spaniards nearby, based on reports from the previous expedition. He paid Indians to find them, and they returned with one man. Jerónimo de Aguilar had been shipwrecked eight years earlier and had lived as a servant among natives called the Mayans. When he saw his fellow countrymen, Aguilar wept with joy. He warned the Spaniards that the natives were fierce fighters. But Cortés was not afraid, and he asked Aguilar to serve as his *interpreter*.

When Cortés sailed on from Cozumel, he landed next near the town of Tabasco. Here the people were not friendly, and in a great battle the Spaniards' guns killed many Tabascans. Still the natives fought. Then, on a signal from Cortés, his *cavalry* (soldiers on horseback) joined the fight. The Tabascans, who had never seen horses, were awestruck, and the Spanish victory was decisive.

To make peace with the powerful strangers who had defeated them, the Tabascans gave Cortés 20 native women. One of them would prove very valuable. Called Doña Marina by the Spaniards, she would eventually make it possible for Cortés to communicate with the Aztecs. Doña Marina spoke both Mayan and *Nahuatl*, the Aztec language. She could translate what the Aztecs said into Mayan, which Aguilar understood. Aguilar could then translate the Mayan into Spanish for Cortés. When Cortés wanted to reply, the process worked in reverse.

The natives of the New World had never seen horses until the Spanish conquistadors arrived in the 16th century. At first, they believed that horses were immortal beings, like gods, that could not be killed.

But Doña Marina's usefulness was not just as an interpreter. She was also a valuable adviser. Without her knowledge of the native peoples' customs, aims, and intentions toward the whites, it is doubtful that Cortés's mission would have succeeded.

The Tabascans offered little wealth, but they did tell of a tribe farther west that had much gold. The explorers sailed on to a place called San Juan de Alua. (This Spanish name was given to the place by an earlier expedition.) The people here were called Totonacs, and their city was called Cempoala. Here Cortés decided to free himself from the authority of the Cuban governor, Velásquez. He resigned from the expedition, and formed his own town. Cortés named the town Vera Cruz ("True Cross").

During their stay in Vera Cruz, Cortés and his men witnessed a common event among the Totonacs. Five Aztec *emissaries* (official messengers) arrived to demand 20 Totonacs as tribute. The people were to be used for the Aztecs' human sacrifices.

Cortés encouraged the Totonacs to take the Aztecs prisoner. But because he was eager to visit the Aztecs, he secretly released two of the emissaries. He told them to return to their emperor, Montezuma, and tell him that he offered friendship. Meanwhile, the Totonacs believed the two emissaries had escaped. They were afraid an Aztec army would arrive any day, and eagerly agreed to support

Cortés when he promised to help defend them.

Montezuma was unsure if Cortés was a god. He sent messengers with gifts of gold and other treasure, hoping the stranger would go away. Cortés sent the messengers and the other three prisoners back, saying he would meet Montezuma soon.

Cortés and a few men then secretly burned their ships. This way his soldiers had no chance of retreat. Cortés believed this would make them fight harder. They would go forward because they could not go back. Then the Spanish army began the long, hard march inland to the Aztec capital. Tenochtitlán was 250 miles from the coast.

Along the way, the Spaniards discovered a large stone wall that marked the boundaries of Tlazcala. The Tlaxcalans were fierce warriors who hated the Aztecs and had managed to remain independent. But they did not trust these strangers. Using

The natives of central Mexico had few reasons to help the Aztecs. For years they had been forced to send their people and goods to Tenochtitlán as tribute. After being defeated by the Spaniards, many of these tribes joined the white men, hoping to rid themselves of Aztec domination.

surprise tactics, they inflicted heavy losses on the Spanish. Finally, after several weeks of fighting, the Tlaxcalans made peace. Cortés made an alliance with them against the hated Aztecs.

The next city Cortés encountered was Cholula. Here the people seemed friendly, but Doña Marina had warned Cortés that a surprise attack was planned by an army of Aztecs waiting outside Cholula. Historians disagree on whether there actually was an Aztec army nearby. But, thus warned, Cortés attacked first. The Spanish and Tlaxcalans massacred thousands of unarmed Cholulans.

When the Spaniards and their native allies arrived at Tenochtitlán, Montezuma welcomed them in peace. They were given a palace, which had belonged to Montezuma's father, to live in. Cortés posted guards and did not allow his men to come and go as they pleased. It was best to be cautious when surrounded by so many people skilled at war.

Montezuma invited the strangers to explore the city with him. The Spanish were amazed at the straight, clean streets. They marveled at the gardens, parks, and plazas. Tenochtitlán even had a zoo! But when they saw religious ceremonies, the Spaniards became sickened. The Aztec priests cut the hearts

The Aztecs' gruesome practice of human sacrifice, as shown here, horrified the Christian Spaniards.

from their living victims to feed the gods "divine water," or blood. The insides of the temples were caked with gore, and skulls and bones numbered in the tens of thousands.

The Spaniards found the Aztecs' religious practices appalling. Finally Cortés decided to stop the human sacrifice. He ordered the fearsome statue of Huitzilopochtli, the Aztecs' patron god, to be destroyed. He also had the Aztec temples scrubbed clean and erected Christian altars in them.

Why did the Aztecs, who had developed a very advanced civilization, practice something as barbaric as human sacrifice? The Aztecs believed that day would not automatically follow night. Night was evil and had to be defeated every day by the Aztec gods. And those gods needed nourishment in the form of human blood to carry on their fight.

Soon after the Spaniards first entered Tenochtitlán, Cortés made Montezuma a prisoner in his own capital. With a squad of soldiers he went to the emperor's palace and informed Montezuma that he could either choose to be killed on the spot or come to live in the Spaniards' borrowed palace as Cortés's "guest." Montezuma wept—realizing, perhaps, that the Aztec Empire would end with his reign, as the prophets had foretold.

But for the average Aztec, life continued as usual. Although many began to resent the strangers' greed and their meddling in Aztec religious practices, Montezuma still seemed to be in charge. Often he could be seen escorting his white-skinned guests around the city. But he was nothing more than a puppet ruler. He seems to have resigned himself to this fate. He even helped the Spaniards, telling them about the Aztec

Empire's workings. All the while Cortés and his men were collecting the emperor's gold and other treasures.

In May of 1520, messengers brought news that more Spaniards had landed in Yucatán. Cortés correctly guessed that they must have been sent by the governor of Cuba, Diego de Velásquez, to arrest him. Leaving some men in Tenochtitlán under the command of Pedro de Alvarado, his assistant, Cortés led the rest of his soldiers toward the coast.

The 900-man force Velásquez had sent was led by a tough leader named Pánfilo de Narváez. Cortés couldn't hope to defeat this army in battle, but he had another plan. He captured several of Narváez's **sentries** and told them about Tenochtitlán's fabulous wealth. Then he released the sentries, who went into their camps and told the stories to their friends. In the middle of the night, Cortés and his men surprised Narváez, capturing him and his guns. Cortés then persuaded Narváez's men to join him and share in the riches they had already heard about.

Cortés had managed to turn a crisis into a huge success. But while he was away dealing with Narváez, trouble had broken out in Tenochtitlán.

Alvarado had given permission for the Aztecs to

The disastrous confusion of la noche triste—*the*
sorrowful night—as the Spanish attempt to escape from
Tenochtitlán secretly was thwarted by angry Aztecs.
Many Spaniards were killed; Cortés barely escaped.

gather for a religious festival. But when he saw thousands of people in the streets, he was afraid they would attack. Alvarado ordered his men to fire on the crowds. The Aztecs were shocked at this unprovoked violence. Already angry at the intruders for their destruction of the temples, the Aztecs fought back. The Spaniards and their Tlaxcalan allies were forced to retreat to their borrowed palace.

When Cortés returned, he found a tense standoff. Alvarado's group was isolated in the palace, and the Aztecs were now refusing to supply them with food. Cortés tried to smooth over the problems, but it was too late. Aztec soldiers surrounded the palace. Cortés brought Montezuma to the palace roof to tell his people to end the fighting. The Aztecs responded by showering Montezuma with stones. One struck the emperor in the head, and three days later he died.

Now desperate, the Spaniards planned to slip out of the city at night with all the treasure they could carry. They built a portable bridge to fill the gaps in the causeway leading to the mainland.

On the night of June 30 the breakout began. At first all went well. But then a woman spotted the Spaniards and cried out an alarm. Aztec warriors poured into the streets and into canoes on the lake.

The portable bridge stuck in a gap and could not be budged. The Spaniards were forced to jump, swim, or in some cases walk over the bodies of their comrades to cross the gaps. Cortés barely escaped. The majority of his men did not, and almost all who survived were wounded. Most of the treasure was lost. Safe on the mainland, Cortés is said to have gazed at the scene and wept. The Spaniards called that night *la noche triste*–the sorrowful night.

For the survivors, though, the ordeal wasn't over. As they hurried to reach the safety of Tlaxcala, an Aztec army of thousands blocked their path through the Valley of Otumba. Cortés led his outnumbered forces into battle. The fighting raged for hours. Finally, in a bold stroke, Cortés and four other horsemen went after the Aztec general, Cihuaca. When they killed him, the Aztecs withdrew. This was their custom when a leader was slain.

The weary Spaniards stumbled to Tlaxcala. Fortunately, the Tlaxcalans still welcomed them and provided food and shelter. They could easily have massacred the weakened Spanish forces.

Cortés's men spent the summer and fall with the Tlaxcalans, nursing their wounds while their leader reorganized his forces. From Vera Cruz, Cortés sent

This Indian depiction of the Battle of Otumba, painted on cloth, shows Cortés killing the Aztec leader Cihuaca.

to Hispaniola for more supplies and men. Having disobeyed the orders of the governor of Cuba, he was officially an outlaw. But Spaniards who had heard of the riches to be won in Mexico eagerly joined him. And they brought horses and guns.

Cortés decided that the way to take Tenochtitlán was by **siege**. To do this he would have to control Lake Texcoco. So he ordered 12 ships to be constructed. The Spaniards supervised and the Tlaxcalans did most of the work. After the ships had been built, they were taken apart. That way they could be carried to the shores of Lake Texcoco and reassembled there. By December 1520, Cortés was ready to return to Tenochtitlán.

What Cortés didn't know was that the Aztecs had been suffering since the defeat of his army. The Europeans had brought the **smallpox** virus to the city. The peoples of the New World had never been exposed to the virus, so they had no **immunity** to it. Aztecs were dying by the thousands from smallpox. Montezuma's brother and successor, Cuitláhuac, was among the first to perish. He was succeeded by Cuauhtémoc, who was determined to fight the Spaniards to the end. But when the Spanish attack came, it came upon a weakened city.

When Cortés's force arrived at Tenochtitlán, they first conquered the suburbs around it. One of their first actions was to destroy the aqueduct that brought the city fresh water. The reassembled ships, which were fitted with cannons, prevented the Aztecs from bringing food and water by canoe. The Spaniards also cut the causeways connecting Tenochtitlán with the mainland. Though their supplies dwindled, the Aztecs fought fiercely. They repelled cavalry attacks with spears tipped with **obsidian** (a black, glassy, volcanic stone) or the metal tips of swords left behind by Spaniards. The Aztecs sacrificed Spanish and Tlaxcalan prisoners, whose dying screams reached Cortés's men. Several times Cortés himself was almost captured.

The siege lasted 60 days, and the fighting was bitter. Finally, the Spaniards were able to enter the city. There the fighting continued in the streets. House by house, street by street, the Spaniards pushed the Aztecs back. Cuauhtémoc refused to surrender, and Cortés ordered that the city be destroyed building by building. Finally, on August 13, 1521, the Spaniards won a decisive battle and captured Cuauhtémoc. Seeing that further resistance was pointless, the last Aztec emperor urged his warriors to surrender. Over 70,000 did so, and the fighting ended. The Tlaxcalans, as was their custom, joyfully looted the once-magnificent city.

Building a
Newer New
World

This native artwork shows Cortés and his Indian allies marching through Mexico. The Spaniards' brutal conquest of the Aztecs would have a long-lasting impact on the region.

4

Having defeated the most warlike of Mexico's peoples, Cortés now had complete control of the region—at least for the time being. He didn't know if he was in trouble for disobeying Velásquez or whether the king of Spain would reward him for his conquests.

But Cortés didn't wait to find out. He immediately ordered his people—Spaniards, natives, and African slaves from Cuba and Hispaniola—to rebuild the demolished city

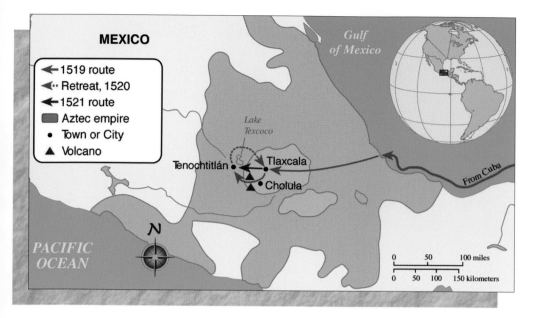

This map shows the size of the Aztec Empire, and the route that Cortés and his men took through Mexico to conquer this powerful empire.

of Tenochtitlán. It would be the capital of the new Spanish colony of New Spain, as the conquistadors had begun calling Mexico. The city was built with stone from Aztec buildings. Tons of lumber and other materials were brought from the mountains.

As a reward for their invaluable help, the Tlaxcalans were to remain free and keep their lands. But other Indians were enslaved. Already weakened by disease, starvation, and war, thousands of natives now died from overwork as they rebuilt the city that today is known as Mexico City.

Cortés had been sending shipments of Aztec gold and treasures back to Spain. Finally, in 1523, he learned that his service was being rewarded. He received a letter from King Charles naming him governor of New Spain. His insubordination against Governor Velásquez had been forgiven, and he was no longer considered an outlaw. Along with this news came the order that the encomienda system, which had led to horrible abuses of natives in other colonies, was not to be introduced into New Spain.

This was a problem. Most of the Aztecs' wealth had been sent back to Spain already. And Cortés had an army of soldiers demanding their share of the riches. Although he personally didn't think the encomienda system was the best way to make his colony prosper, he didn't want his soldiers to rebel. Reluctantly, Cortés went against the king's orders and established some encomiendas to pay his men.

Eventually, King Charles accepted the land grants Cortés had made. But he declared that these encomiendas would not be **hereditary** (passed from parent to child). Both Charles and Cortés seemed to hope that the evils of the system would not be transplanted from other Spanish colonies to New Spain. But this is in fact what did happen.

Cortés wanted to get the farming of the new colony started. Sheep, cattle, pigs, chickens, and horses were brought from Europe. Wheat, cotton, and other crops were planted. Gold and silver mines were dug, using Indian labor.

In 1522, Cortés's wife Catalina arrived in Mexico City. She died shortly thereafter. Many people believed that Cortés had poisoned her. After all, he already had some children by other women. One of these women was a daughter of Montezuma. (Also, Doña Marina would bear him a son in 1525.)

Cortés was now a wealthy man. He owned enormous estates near Cuernavaca, south of Mexico City. But he was not a farmer. He still hungered to explore. In 1523 he began sending out new expeditions to explore other parts of New Spain. For years Europeans had hoped to find a sea passage through the lands of the New World to China. Cortés sent ships along the coast to look for such a passage.

Pedro de Alvarado, who explored the southern regions, founded the city of Oaxaca. Another officer named Cristóbal de Olid went west and reached the Pacific, then sailed along that coast to explore.

Cortés told the men on these voyages of discovery to treat the natives they encountered well. But they didn't always obey this order. The Spaniards still dreamed of untold riches, and when natives said they had no gold, the Spaniards often assumed they were lying. Greed for gold often led the Spanish invaders to torture and kill natives and loot their towns. (Cortés himself tortured the captured Aztec leader Cuauhtémoc. Cortés hoped the prisoner would tell him where the vast golden treasure lost on *la noche triste* was hidden, but Cuauhtémoc never did. To this day, none of it has been found.)

When Olid traveled south, into present-day Honduras, he decided to start his own colony, much as Cortés himself had done. Olid made a partnership with Velásquez to divide up the gold, and they planned to deny Cortés a share of any wealth he found. As soon as he heard this news, Cortés sent a force to punish Olid.

After a small army was sent to find Olid, Cortés decided he should hunt down the troublemaker himself. He gathered an army and set out from Mexico City. To prevent a possible uprising in his absence, he took Cuauhtémoc along.

The journey would be perhaps the longest and most difficult of Cortés's career. The rainforests were almost impassable, there were 50 rivers to

King Charles I of Spain appreciated the Aztec gold that Cortés sent from the New World, but he was concerned because of the conquistador's reputation for flaunting authority. In 1526, he ordered Cortés to return to Spain.

cross, and the footpaths through the mountains were narrow and treacherous.

As the army ran out of food and supplies, rumors started that the Indians in the group planned to rebel. Cortés questioned Cuauhtémoc, who denied any such plans. The Aztec leader was hanged by Cortés anyway. Even some of the Spaniards believed this was a cruel and unfair punishment.

After 18 difficult months, Cortés and his army reached Honduras, only to find that the trip had been a waste of time. The rebellious Olid had already been defeated and killed by the force Cortés had sent earlier. So Cortés and his army returned north by sea and arrived home much more quickly.

But while Cortés was on this two-year chase, the king's agent in Mexico City, Gonzalo de Salazar, had seized power. A cruel and unwise leader, Salazar had so infuriated the native people that they had rebelled. As a result, Cortés was hailed by the Spaniards and even by some Indians as a hero when he finally returned. The people, Spanish and Indian alike, hoped he would restore order.

To the native peoples, Cortés was their ruler. He had conquered the old kings and built a new city on the ashes of their old capital. But Velásquez and his many supporters did not see it that way. They did not think Cortés had any authority to be ruler. After all, he had disobeyed Velásquez, who had been appointed by the king and was Cortés's **superior**. In 1526 they convinced King Charles to revoke Cortés's title of governor of New Spain.

King Charles also ordered Cortés to return to Spain. As soon as the situation in New Spain settled, he set sail. After a lifetime of exploring and conquering, he was going home to answer to his king.

Cortés's exploits in Mexico made him one of the richest men in Spain. However, he wasted much of his fortune in attempts to find even more gold exploring the New World.

Homecoming 5

When Cortés returned to Spain in 1528, he was a great lord. He brought with him not only treasures for the king, but also Mexican nobles (including a son of Montezuma), and exotic animals such as tropical birds, anteaters, ocelots (small wildcats), jaguars, and armadillos. Because of his vast landholdings in the New World, Cortés was probably the second-wealthiest man in Spain, after the king. And the tales of his daring adventures and his conquest of the fierce Aztecs had made him a hero in the country of his birth. He was welcomed with almost royal fanfare.

As for King Charles, he was undoubtedly grateful to Cortés, and rightfully so. This conquistador had expanded Charles's kingdom many times over and had added untold amounts of gold to the royal treasury. But years of hearing reports from Velásquez and others about Cortés's rebelliousness had made Charles suspicious. He thought Cortés might one day rebel against him, so he refused to reinstate him as governor of New Spain.

The king did make Cortés captain-general and even gave him the high noble title of Marquis of the Valley of Oaxaca. But Cortés could not win back the governorship.

While in Spain, Cortés married a Spanish noblewoman, Doña Juana de Zúñiga. Finally, with the king's confirmation of his vast landholdings in hand, Cortés and his second wife returned to New Spain in 1530. He settled in Cuernavaca, where he spent much of his time.

Cortés's holdings in New Spain included some 50 towns and villages. In addition to silver and gold mines, he owned farms that grew cotton and sugar and supported sheep, cattle, and horses. There was surely much work to do there. But Cortés still longed to explore. He wanted to find Cíbola, a legendary land with seven cities built of pure gold.

Cortés used the wealth from his huge estates to pay for his expeditions. He founded the Pacific coast town of Acapulco, now a famous resort city, as a ship-building station. In 1532, Cortés sent two ships to explore the Pacific coast of what is now Mexico. Only one returned, and it brought no important information. In 1534, Cortés sent two more ships, but both were lost. Finally, Cortés decided to explore the area himself.

According to a 16th century Spanish legend, after the Moors invaded Spain, seven Christian bishops took their people on a voyage west. When they found land, the refugees established seven cities that soon became very rich—the fabled Seven Cities of Gold.

In May 1535, Cortés set out with 400 soldiers and 100 horses on three ships. He sailed north and reached the southern tip of what is now Baja California. There he stayed, intending to establish a settlement, and sent his ships back for more men and supplies. Only one ship returned. He set out to find the other two, which he succeeded in doing. But in the meantime, his men ashore were nearly starving, and the natives who lived nearby knew nothing of the legendary Seven Cities of Cíbola.

Still, Cortés continued the search, sending ships back for supplies and sending exploring parties north. They found nothing important. Finally, after a year, everyone returned to Mexico.

These expeditions cost Cortés a lot of money. Because he did not find riches, Cortés was forced to sell many of his lands to pay his debts. Still determined to explore, he decided to try to win the king's favor. In 1540, he returned to Spain once more.

When Cortés arrived, King Charles was away fighting a war in the Netherlands. It was a year before the king returned. Then Charles decided to launch a war against the Muslim city of Algiers, in North Africa. Cortés and two of his sons volunteered. Cortés hoped that he could win the king's favor by succeeding in battle.

He sailed for Algiers with Charles's forces, but the Spanish fleet was destroyed by a huge storm. Cortés was among the lucky few to survive. He offered to lead the handful of remaining soldiers against Algiers, but the Spanish generals dismissed his foolhardy plan. He would not get a chance to win Charles's favor.

On December 2, 1547, sick and far from his adopted home, Hernando Cortés died in a town near Seville, Spain. He was buried in Seville, although he wished to be buried in Mexico City. In 1566 his remains were transported there and reburied in a church.

Cortés's remains were moved several times in the 1700s, as city leaders built monuments to honor his memory. In the early 1800s, Mexico won its independence from Spain. In the anti-Spanish atmosphere of the times, some people threatened to dig up Cortés's remains and burn them publicly. But the remains were not found; they had been removed from the grave and hidden. In 1947, Cortés's remains were found in the church where he had originally been buried, but not in the same spot. The church, which had fallen into disrepair, was restored, and Cortés's remains were reburied yet again.

Cortés's conquest of the Aztecs had marked the beginning of the vibrant Mexican culture we know today. That culture is a mix of two civilizations: Spanish and Indian. Just as Mexican culture combines Spanish and native traditions, so the majority of Mexican people are of mixed Spanish and Indian ancestry, or **mestizos**. One of the first mestizos was

The ruins of the Aztec culture, such as the great Pyramid
of the Sun, are popular tourist attractions today.

the son of Cortés and Doña Marina, the native woman who was the conquistador's interpreter, adviser, and longtime companion.

Today Mexico City is one of the largest cities in the world. But it has no monument to Hernando Cortés, the man who founded the city. Mexico City does have a statue of the Aztec king Cuauhtémoc, though. And every year, costumed dancers perform around it to commemorate Cuauhtémoc's bravery and defiance of the Spanish conquerors. For many Mexicans, Cuauhtémoc, not Cortés, is the great hero of the conquest.

Why do Mexicans have mixed feelings about Cortés? Probably some of it is due to his ruthless and often brutal treatment of the Indians. And some of it, no doubt, has to do with the injustices that grew out of the Spanish colonization. The encomienda system, which Cortés introduced into Mexico, ensured that wealth would be concentrated in the hands of a few people of Spanish descent. Meanwhile, the native peoples, now landless, would toil under horrible conditions and remain poor. The gap between the landed rich and the landless poor remained a feature of Mexican society centuries after Cortés had died.

Yet it is unfair to blame Cortés for all the injustices that occurred in Mexico after his conquest. And though by today's standards he was a ruthless and greedy man, he was also a fearless explorer, an inspiring leader, a clever strategist, and a brilliant general.

Chronology

1325 Aztecs found city of Tenochtitlán.

1485 Hernando Cortés born in the province of Extremadura, Spain.

1492 Columbus arrives in Hispaniola.

1499 Cortés, age 14, goes to the University of Salamanca to study law.

1503 Montezuma becomes Aztec leader; Spanish slave trade begins in the New World.

1504 Cortés travels to Hispaniola, is granted land, and becomes a sugar planter.

1511 Accompanies Diego Velásquez to Cuba; is granted land there and marries Catalina Xuárez.

1518 Begins preparing for an expedition to the Yucatán Peninsula (in present-day Mexico).

1519 Lands in Yucatán, burns ships after arrival; meets Jerónimo de Aguilar, and is given Doña Marina as a gift; founds town of Vera Cruz; enters Aztec capital city after defeating Tlaxcalans and other native groups; takes emperor Montezuma prisoner; defeats Spanish force sent to capture him.

1520 Fighting breaks out with Aztecs in Tenochtitlán; Montezuma killed by his own people, and Cortés retreats with heavy losses on the night of June 30; leads survivors to Tlaxcala after winning battle of Otumba; prepares for siege of Tenochtitlán; smallpox rages among the Aztecs, killing Montezuma's successor, Cuitláhuac.

1521 Cortés besieges Tenochtitlán, defeats Aztecs and destroys city; takes last Aztec emperor, Cuauhtémoc, prisoner; builds Mexico City atop the ruins of Tenochtitlán.

1522 Wife Catalina dies after going to Mexico City; rumors circulate that Cortés poisoned her.

1523 Appointed governor of colony of New Spain (Mexico).

1524 Marches through jungles to Honduras to punish a mutinous subordinate, Christóbal de Olid.

1525 Executes Cuauhtémoc on suspicion of treachery. Doña Marina gives birth to Cortés's son.

1526 Returns to Mexico City to find his enemies have convinced King Charles to strip him of the governorship of New Spain.

1528 Returns to Spain to meet with King Charles.

1529 Is appointed captain-general of New Spain and Marquis of Valley of Oaxaca. Marries Doña Juana de Zúñiga.

1530 Returns to New Spain and lives on estate in Cuernavaca.

1532 Founds town of Acapulco, builds ships to explore Pacific coast.

1535 Explores as far north as Baja California.

1540 Returns to Spain.

1541 Volunteers, with his two sons, to fight for King Charles in Algiers, Africa; survives loss of Spanish fleet.

1547 Dies near Seville and is buried in Spain.

1566 Remains brought to New Spain and buried in Mexico City.

Glossary

aqueduct—a structure for carrying flowing water.

causeway—a raised road over a body of water.

cavalry—soldiers who fight on horseback.

conquistadors—Spanish soldiers who conquered native tribes.

emissary—a person sent on a mission on behalf of a leader; official messenger.

encomenderos—landowners under the encomienda system.

encomienda system—a system by which land and natives were given to conquistadors and colonists in Spain's New World colonies; in return for the natives' labor, the encomenderos were supposed to provide them with food and a Christian education.

hereditary—property that is passed from generation to generation.

human sacrifice—the ritual killing of human beings in order to please or gain favors from the gods.

immunity—a natural protection from disease. The natives of the New World were not immune to diseases carried by European explorers, so they were at greater risk of dying from the diseases.

interpreter—a person who helps two people who speak different languages to communicate by translating what they are saying.

mercenaries—soldiers for hire.

mestizos—people of mixed Spanish and Indian ancestry.

Moors–Arabs from North Africa who invaded Spain in the
eighth century. Because the Moors followed Islam, they
were involved in a series of bloody wars with the Christian people of Spain and the rest of Europe. The Moors
were forced out of Spain in 1492.

Nahuatl–the native language of the Aztecs.

obsidian–volcanic glass that could be made into razor-sharp
pieces; the Aztecs used obsidian for blades and points
on spears.

peninsula–a land area surrounded on three sides by water.

plantation–a large farm or estate where plants and trees are
cultivated.

province–a region of a country, usually separated from other
provinces by geographical or political boundaries.

sentry–a soldier on guard.

siege–a military tactic that involves surrounding and cutting off
supplies to a city in order to weaken its defenders.

smallpox–a disease, caused by a virus, that devastated the
Aztecs after contact with Cortes's group.

suburbs–outlying parts of a city.

superior–someone of higher rank or position to whom a person
owes obedience.

tribute–goods or services collected from a conquered people by
the conquerors.

Further Reading

DeAngelis, Therese. *The Native Americans and the Spanish.* Philadelphia: Chelsea House, 1997.

Flowers, Sarah. *The Age of Exploration.* San Diego: Lucent Books, 1999.

Fritz, Jean. *Around the World in a Hundred Years.* New York: G. P. Putnam's Sons, 1994.

Haworth-Maden, Clare. *Explorers and Exploration: Latin America* (vol. 5). Danbury, CT: Grolier Educational, 1998.

Hunter, Nigel. *The Expeditions of Cortés.* New York: Bookwright Press, 1990.

Larsen, Anita. *Montezuma's Missing Treasure.* New York: Crestwood House, 1992.

Lilley, Stephen R. *The Conquest of Mexico.* San Diego: Lucent Books, 1997.

Mathews, Sally Schofer. *The Sad Night.* New York: Clarion Books, 1994.

Stein, R. Conrad. *Hernando Cortés.* Chicago: Children's Press, 1991.

Picture Credits

GINA DE ANGELIS earned her B.A. in theater and history and her M.A. in history. She is the author of several young adult books in history, biography, and other subjects, and has written plays and screenplays as well. She lives in Williamsburg, Virginia, with her daughter and pet gerbils.